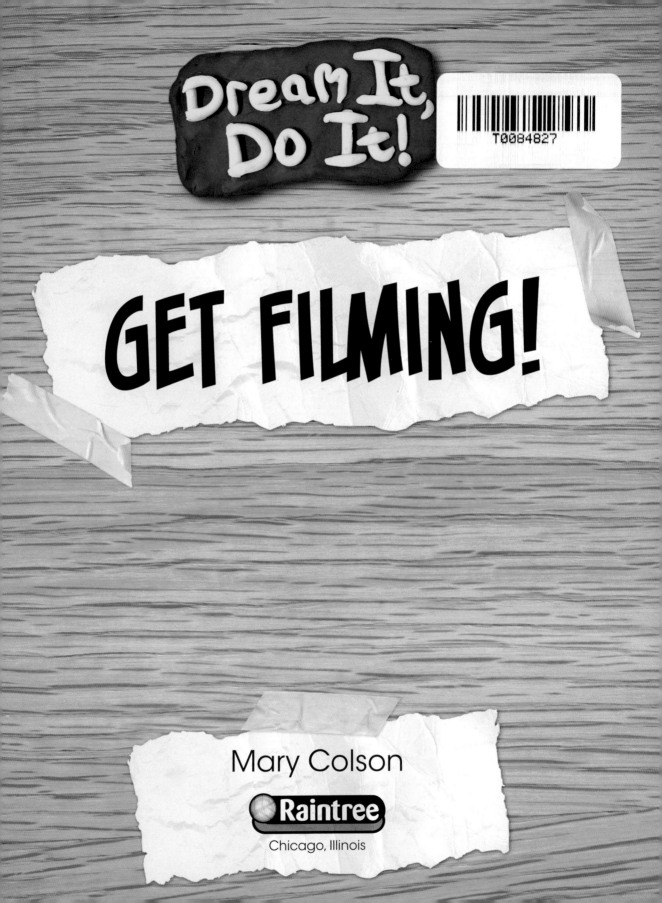

Dream It, Do It!

GET FILMING!

Mary Colson

Raintree

Chicago, Illinois

Edited by Rebecca Rissman, Dan Nunn, and Helen Cox Cannons
Designed by Steve Mead
Original illustrations © Capstone Global Library, Ltd
Picture research by Ruth Blair
Production by Vicki Fitzgerald
Originated by Capstone Global Library, Ltd
Printed and bound in China by CTPS

17 16 15 14 13
10 9 8 7 6 5 4 3 2 1

Library of Congress Cataloging-in-Publication Data
Colson, Mary.
 Get filming! / Mary Colson.
     p. cm.—(Dream it, do it!)
Includes bibliographical references and index.
ISBN 978-1-4109-6265-2 (hb)—ISBN 978-1-4109-6270-6 (pb) 1. Motion
picture authorship—Vocational guidance. 2. Motion pictures—
Production and direction—Vocational guidance. I. Title.

PN1996.C765 2013
791.4302'3—dc23   2013017425

Acknowledgments
The author and publisher are grateful to the following for permission
to reproduce copyright material: Alamy pp.5 (© Photos 12), 25 (© AF
archive); Capstone Publishers pp. 26–29 (© Karon Dubke); Corbis pp.
12 (© Mark Rightmire/ZUMA Press), 16 (© Etienne George/Sygma);
Getty Images pp. 6 (Radius Images), 13 (Betsie Van der Meer), 14
(WireImage), 23 (Siri Stafford); Shutterstock pp. 4 (© Klemzy), 8 (©
Khakimullin Aleksandr), 9 (© vovan), 10 left (© Albert Ziganshin), 10 right
(© David Evison), 11 (© Yuri Arcurs), 15 left (© van Ponomarev), 15 right
(© ppart), 17 left (© pichayasri), 17 right (© Christos Georghiou), 18 (©
Strejman), 19 (© Goodluz), 20 (© absolut), 20, 21 (© ostill). Incidental
photographs reproduced with permission of Shutterstock.

Cover photograph of a boy holding a video camera reproduced with
permission of Corbis (© David Deas/DK Stock).

We would like to thank Chris and Kristen Barker for their invaluable help
in the preparation of this book.

Every effort has been made to contact copyright holders of any
material reproduced in this book. Any omissions will be rectified in
subsequent printings if notice is given to the publisher.

All the Internet addresses (URLs) given in this book were valid at the time
of going to press. However, due to the dynamic nature of the Internet,
some addresses may have changed, or sites may have changed or
ceased to exist since publication. While the author and publisher regret
any inconvenience this may cause readers, no responsibility for any
such changes can be accepted by either the author or the publisher.

CONTENTS

Some words are shown in bold, **like this**. You can find out what they mean by looking in the glossary.

BE A FILMMAKER!

Filmmakers work with cameras, **scripts**, actors, **props**, and music to create film magic. If you dream about making films of your own, you could become a filmmaker!

Filmmakers are creative, imaginative, and want to tell good stories. You can make a film about anything that you like. It doesn't have to be a made-up story—you could create a film about a typical day in your life.

FILM YOURSELF

Filmmakers tell stories that they hope people will want to see. What do you think would make a good story? Thinking about your own life may give you some good ideas.

Activity

Stand in front of a mirror and pretend you are looking into a camera lens. You can pretend to be someone famous, someone you know, or you can be yourself. Watch how your face moves and changes as you speak.

MOVIE MIND MAPPING

What kinds of films do you enjoy? Comedy? Action? Fantasy? Filmmakers always start with an idea of the type of film they want to make, and then they work from there. After recording their ideas, filmmakers think about how to make the story as exciting and entertaining as possible.

Activity

Start a filmmaker's **journal** and write down all of your wonderful story and character ideas. Don't cross any ideas out—they might be useful later!

Ideas

set at school?
sports club?
tough coach?
injury?
team win?
celebrations!

PLOTTING PLOTS

All films need a good **plot**, or story. What's your plot going to be? Is it going to be about good winning over evil? Or about someone solving a problem and learning something important? A filmmaker plots out every detail of his or her film.

Activity

Imagine that you're planning a film with a hero and a villain in it. Plan out your plot by answering the following questions in your **journal**.

1. Where and when does your story take place?
2. Who is your hero?
3. Who is your villain?
4. What happens when they meet?

WRITING THE SCRIPT

All films have **scripts**. Scripts tell the actors and actresses what to say and where to stand. They also describe a **scene**, or place, where the action happens.

Activity

Have a script reading! Ask an adult to help you find the script of a film that you like. Get your friends to read different parts out loud.

JESSE'S face.

JESSE
(quiet)
Year later, she died.
(soft)
We went up that hill with him, too.

Troubled silence from MRS. LOWE as she looks long at the lonely figure of LANE standing motionless at the bend of the river...and we:

Thank you up and over another angle

back to JESSE watching

DISSOLVE TO:

EXT. CAMP - NIGHT

Night is near over as we from high atop th ead qui

A script reading with friends can be fun.

CHARACTERS, COSTUMES, AND CASTING

Filmmakers need to choose the right characters for their film. They need to dress the characters in the right way. For example, evil characters often wear black, and good characters wear white.

Voldemort, Harry Potter Films

Activity

Draw outlines of people in your **journal**. Create a **collage** of your characters by cutting out pictures from magazines. Think about how you want them to look and the clothes they should wear. It might help you to think of which real-life actors and actresses you would **cast** to play your characters.

ON LOCATION: SET DESIGN

Some filmmakers build **sets**, or stages. Others film outdoors, or in famous places. Where do you want your film set? In a forest? In a new world? In a castle? Think creatively!

Activity

Take a cardboard box and cut away one side. Gather together poster board, paint, and pens to create a mini set!

Using cut-out figures (or dolls) as your characters, move them around the set as you speak their lines. Which part of the set works best?

MUSIC AND ATMOSPHERE

Music is used in films to create different moods and emotions. Think about scary moments in films—such as a shark attack—where the music adds to the **atmosphere**.

Activity

Choose five pieces of music that you think create different moods, such as scary, happy, or sad. Make a **soundtrack** of these five pieces.

Play your pieces to a friend. Ask them how the music makes them feel. Do they agree with you?

CAMERAS AND ANGLES

We don't always see film action from the same angle. Sometimes we see the view from above, and sometimes we see a **close-up**. Filmmakers experiment with different camera angles to keep the audience interested.

Activity

Use a camera to practice zooming in on an object. If you don't have a camera, use your hands to make an imaginary lens to look through. Try filming the object from above, the side, and below.

FILMING AND EDITING

Filmmakers make their movies and then **edit** them. Editing is when parts of the film are pieced together or cut out, or a camera angle is changed. This is done to make the best film possible for the audience to enjoy.

Activity

After you've finished filming a **scene**, watch it back. Do you need all of it, or can you cut parts out?

Show your film to an audience. What is their opinion? What changes do they suggest?

MAKING A TRAILER

All films have trailers. Trailers are short advertisements for the film that are shown to audiences. The filmmaker hopes that the audience will be hooked and want to see the whole film.

Activity

Choose three key moments from your film. Use these moments to make your trailer. Don't forget to show or say what the film is called and when it will be ready to watch.

Show your trailer to an audience. Are they hooked? Do they want to see the whole film?

LIGHTS, CAMERA...

A **storyboard** shows the story action **scene** by scene in pictures and notes. Filmmakers use storyboards to help them track the details of the story as they film. Follow these simple steps to create your own film storyboard.

1. Get a large piece of paper, a ruler, and a pencil.

2. Draw eight boxes in two rows of four, one row on top of the other.

3. Rule a line either above or below each row of boxes. This will be your box for notes on each picture.

...ACTION!

4. Now you're ready to create!

5. In the first box, draw your first **scene**. Think about the setting, the time of day, and the characters in it.

6. Add any notes about what the characters are saying in the little box below the picture.

7. Do this for every box until your story is told.

8. If you want, you can color in your picture to show the mood of the scene.

GLOSSARY

atmosphere mood or feeling of your work

cast choose an actor or actress to play a part in a film

close-up zoomed-in view of something

collage picture made by sticking different materials and pictures onto paper

edit piece together, cut, or change part of a film

journal written record of a person's thoughts and experiences

plot storyline of a book, play, or film

prop object that actors and actresses use to help tell a story

scene place or setting where part of a film happens

script written words of a film

set scenery for a film

soundtrack music chosen to be used in a film

storyboard outline of a film in pictures

FIND OUT MORE

Books

Grabham, Tim. *Movie Maker: The Ultimate Guide to Making Films.* Somerville, Mass.: Candlewick, 2010.

Quijano, Jonathan. *Make Your Movie* (series). Mankato, Minn.: Capstone, 2012.

Web sites

FactHound offers a safe, fun way to find Internet sites related to this book. All of the sites on FactHound have been researched by our staff.

Here's all you do:

Visit www.facthound.com

Type in this code: 9781410962652

INDEX